ENCOURAGEMENT FOR

MEN

2008 by Barbour Publishing, Inc.

Compiled by Kate E. Schmelzer.

ISBN 978-1-60260-204-5

Some material previously published in *365 Inspirational Quotes* and *365 Days of Hope,* published by Barbour Publishing, Inc

Scripture taken from the HOLY BIBLE, NEW INTERNATIONAL VERSION®. NIV®. Copyright © 1973, 1978, 1984 by Internation Bible Society. Used by permission of Zondervan. All rights reserved.

Cover Photograph: Minoru Kida/Amana Images/Getty Images

Published by Barbour Publishing, Inc., P.O. Box 719, Uhrichsville, Ohio 44683, www.barbourbooks.com

Our mission is to publish and distribute inspirational products offering exceptional value and biblical encouragement to the masses.

ecpa Member of the
Evangelical Christian
Publishers Association

Printed in China.

ENCOURAGEMENT FOR

MEN

BARBOUR
PUBLISHING

I find the great thing in this world is not so much where we stand, as in what direction we are moving. To reach the port of heaven, we must sail sometimes with the wind and sometimes against it—but we must sail, and not drift—nor lie at anchor.

OLIVER WENDELL HOLMES

THE BEST WAY TO ENJOY LIFE
IS TO TAKE EACH DAY AT A TIME.

My God goes before me in battle.
His arms are strong and wide. They protect me
through my day. Whatever I do, I do it with confidence—
I know I am on the winning side.

"For I know the plans I have for you," declares the Lord,
*"plans to prosper you and not to harm you,
plans to give you hope and a future."*

JEREMIAH 29:11

THERE IS A FRIEND WHO STICKS
CLOSER THAN A BROTHER.

PROVERBS 18:24

I have held many things in my hands and lost them all;
but the things I have placed in God's hands,
those I always possess.

EARLINE STEELBURG

PHYSICAL STRENGTH IS NOT ALWAYS
THE BEST PROTECTION.
OFTEN, COURAGE AND
A BIT OF INTELLECT ARE.

*All God's glory and beauty come from within,
and there He delights to dwell. His visits there are frequent,
His conversation sweet, His comforts refreshing,
His peace passing all understanding.*

THOMAS à KEMPIS

Hope means hoping when things are hopeless,
or it is no virtue at all. . . . As long as matters
are really hopeful, hope is mere flattery or platitude;
it is only when everything is hopeless
that hope begins to be a strength.

G. K. CHESTERTON

"Show me, O Lord, my life's end and the number of my days; let me know how fleeting is my life. You have made my days a mere handbreadth; the span of my years is as nothing before you. Each man's life is but a breath. Man is a mere phantom as he goes to and fro: He bustles about, but only in vain; he heaps up wealth, not knowing who will get it. But now, Lord, what do I look for? My hope is in you."

PSALM 39:4-7

SONS ARE A HERITAGE FROM THE LORD,
CHILDREN A REWARD FROM HIM.

PSALM 127:3

*Pray daily. It's the best way to hear
God's voice in a world of deafening noise.*

WHEN YOU NEED HELP, ADMIT IT.
IT WILL OPEN YOU UP TO A WORLD OF NEW
ACCOMPLISHMENTS YOU CAN'T ACHIEVE ALONE.

INSPIRATION COMES AT THE STRANGEST TIMES.
ARM YOURSELF! KEEP A SMALL NOTEPAD, A
PENCIL, AND YOUR IMAGINATION READY.

We grow great by dreams. . . .
[We] see things in the soft haze of a spring day
or in the red fire of a long winter's evening. Some of
us let these great dreams die, but others nourish and protect
them; nurse them through bad days till they bring them to
the sunshine and light which comes always to those who
sincerely hope that their dreams will come true.

WOODROW WILSON

Be patient. People journey at different paces.
Examine yourself and see where you might
need to slow down or speed up.

THIS IS GOOD, AND PLEASES GOD OUR SAVIOR,
WHO WANTS ALL MEN TO BE SAVED AND
TO COME TO A KNOWLEDGE OF THE TRUTH.

1 TIMOTHY 2:3-4

I PRAISE GOD FOR WAKING ME THIS MORNING.
I CAN'T WAIT TO DISCOVER WHAT
TODAY'S PLAN HOLDS FOR ME.

Asking for forgiveness is more than saying, "I'm sorry." It's acknowledging the wrong and praying for the strength to not make the same mistake twice.

I waited patiently for the LORD; he turned to me and heard my cry. He lifted me out of the slimy pit, out of the mud and mire; he set my feet on a rock and gave me a firm place to stand. He put a new song in my mouth, a hymn of praise to our God. Many will see and fear and put their trust in the LORD.

PSALM 40:1-3

DON'T SPEND SO MUCH TIME AT YOUR WORK
THAT YOU FAIL TO SEE THE PURPOSE BEHIND IT.

WATCH THE WAY YOU WALK. NOT WITH YOUR HEAD HELD HIGH ABOVE OTHERS, BUT NOT WITH YOUR HEAD DOWN AND YOUR EYES ON THE GROUND, EITHER. WALK HUMBLY SO THAT YOU CAN SEE WHERE YOU ARE GOING.

Help me spread my fragrance everywhere I go.
Flood my spirit with Thy spirit and life.
Penetrate and possess my whole being
so utterly that all my life may
only be a radiance of Thine.

JOHN HENRY NEWMAN

*The human heart has hidden treasure, in secret kept,
in silence sealed; the thoughts, the hopes, the dreams,
the pleasure, whose charms were broken if revealed.*

CHARLOTTE BRONTË

TROUBLE MIGHT BE AN OPPORTUNITY TO
SHOW OTHERS THE BEST WAY TO HANDLE IT.

Late have I loved You, O beauty so ancient and so new. Late have I loved You! You were within me while I have gone outside to seek You. Unlovely myself, I rushed towards all those lovely things You had made. And always You were with me.

AUGUSTINE

GOD'S WAYS SEEM DARK, BUT SOON OR LATE,
THEY TOUCH THE SHINING HILLS OF DAY.

JOHN GREENLEAF WHITTIER

NO WINTER LASTS FOREVER;
NO SPRING SKIPS ITS TURN.

HAL BORLAND

The Spirit of the Sovereign LORD is on me, because the LORD has anointed me to preach good news to the poor. He has sent me to bind up the brokenhearted, to proclaim freedom for the captives and release from darkness for the prisoners, to proclaim the year of the LORD's favor.

ISAIAH 61:1-2

FOCUS ON YOUR GOD-GIVEN GIFTS
AND ALLOW THEM TO BECOME STRONG
FOR HIS KINGDOM.

*We are so preciously loved by God
that we cannot even comprehend it.
No created being can ever know how much
and how sweetly and tenderly God loves them.*

JULIAN OF NORWICH

Even youths grow tired and weary, and young men stumble and fall; but those who hope in the LORD will renew their strength. They will soar on wings like eagles; they will run and not grow weary, they will walk and not be faint.

ISAIAH 40:30-31

OUR DAYS CAN FEEL MUCH
LIKE A ROCKY STORM AT SEA.
BE SURE YOU HAVE A FIRM ANCHOR,
OR YOU MIGHT FLOAT FAR AWAY FROM HOME.

A MAN SHOULD CARE FOR WHAT HE HAS—
NOT OUT OF SHEER POSSESSION,
BUT BECAUSE HE IS THANKFUL FOR IT.

Now in Christ Jesus you who once were far away have been brought near through the blood of Christ.

EPHESIANS 2:13

Everything which relates to God is infinite.
We must therefore, while we keep our hearts humble, keep
our aims high. Our highest services are indeed but finite,
imperfect. But as God is unlimited in goodness,
He should have our ultimate love.

HANNAH MORE

TIME'S A GREAT TEACHER;
WHO CAN LIVE WITHOUT HOPE?

CARL SANDBURG

Shake a person's hand today. Acknowledging another with an affirmative touch might be just what he or she needs.

OPTIMISM IS THE FAITH THAT LEADS TO
ACHIEVEMENT. NOTHING CAN BE DONE
WITHOUT HOPE OR CONFIDENCE.

HELEN KELLER

CHEER FOR OTHERS. A LITTLE ENCOURAGEMENT
WILL GO A LONG WAY FOR THEIR HEART AND YOURS.

Of all the forces that make for a better world, none is so indispensable, none so powerful, as hope.

CHARLES SAWYER

The smallest bit of obedience opens heaven,
and the deepest truths of God immediately become ours.

OSWALD CHAMBERS

WALKING WITH GOD MEANS GOING IN
THE DIRECTION HE IS GOING—
FULL SPEED AHEAD.

Communion with God is a great sea that fits every bend in the shore of human need.

HARRY EMERSON FOSDICK

TAKE SOME TIME TO RELAX. PLAN A DAY
OR WEEKEND RETREAT TO SPEND SOME TIME
ENJOYING A CHILDHOOD HOBBY.

*God's Spirit moves throughout
the earth and can be called upon.
We are never truly alone.*

ENCOURAGING WORDS MAY BE DIFFICULT
FOR SOME—BUT THEY SPEAK
DIRECTLY TO THE HEART.

*For in the true nature of things,
if we will rightly consider, every green tree is
far more glorious than if it were
made of gold and silver.*

MARTIN LUTHER

"COME WITH ME BY YOURSELVES TO
A QUIET PLACE AND GET SOME REST."

MARK 6:31

MONEY ISN'T EVERYTHING. YOU DIDN'T BRING IT
WITH YOU, AND YOU CAN'T TAKE IT WITH YOU.
SPEND IT WHILE YOU ARE HERE, BUT SPEND IT WISELY.

*It seems to me we can never give up
longing and wishing while we are alive.
There are certain things we feel to
be beautiful and good, and we
must hunger for them.*

GEORGE ELIOT

God's care for us is more watchful and more tender than the care of any human father could possibly be.

HANNAH WHITALL SMITH

TO BECOME TRULY GREAT, ONE HAS TO STAND WITH PEOPLE, NOT ABOVE THEM.

CHARLES DE MONTESQUIEU

NOTHING GREAT IN THE WORLD HAS EVER
BEEN ACCOMPLISHED WITHOUT PASSION.

HEBBEL

The heart might be described by doctors as a bodily organ that pumps, but it is so much more for God's children. It is the home of God.

Trails. . .may come in abundance.
But they cannot penetrate into the sanctuary
of the soul when it is settled in God,
and we may dwell in perfect peace.

HANNAH WHITALL SMITH

"DO NOT FEAR, FOR I AM WITH YOU;
DO NOT BE DISMAYED, FOR I AM YOUR GOD."

ISAIAH 41:10

WHO WOULD HAVE THOUGHT THAT JESUS'
CLOSEST EARTHLY FRIENDSHIPS WOULD
COME FROM SUCH DIVERSE MEN?

I will praise you, O Lord, with all my heart. . . .
[I] will praise your name for your love and your
faithfulness, for you have exalted above
all things your name and your word.

Psalm 138:1-2

BE SUCH A PERSON, AND LIVE SUCH A LIFE,
THAT IF EVERYONE WERE SUCH AS YOU,
AND EVERY LIFE A LIFE SUCH AS YOURS,
THIS EARTH WOULD BE GOD'S PARADISE.

PHILLIPS BROOKS

*Our world has seen thousands
of very powerful leaders.
Whether doing good or bad in their time,
each carried the opportunity to leave a legacy
for the generations that followed.*

*I still find each day too short for all
the thoughts I want to think, all the walks
I want to take, all the books I want to read,
and all the friends I want to see. The longer
I live, the more my mind dwells upon the
beauty and the wonder of the world.*

JOHN BURROUGHS

HOPE IS THE FEELING WE HAVE THAT THE
FEELING WE HAVE IS NOT PERMANENT.

MIGNON McLAUGHLIN

Real love goes beyond feelings such as "I deserve,"
"Give me," and "I want."
Real love begins with a sacrifice.

EVERYTHING THAT IS DONE IN THE WORLD
IS DONE BY HOPE.

MARTIN LUTHER

THROW YOUR HEART OUT IN FRONT OF YOU.
AND RUN AHEAD TO CATCH IT.

ARABIAN PROVERB

The power I have comes not from me but from the One who made me. Through Him, even my weaknesses become strengths.

THINK WHERE THE WORLD WOULD BE
IF WE SUPERSIZED OUR GENEROSITY.

Sometimes it's in silence that we have the ability to hear God's voice—not in a loud thunderstorm, but in a gentle whisper.

THE PAGE OF LIFE THAT HAD SPREAD OUT BEFORE ME
WAS DULL AND COMMONPLACE ONLY BECAUSE
I HAD NOT FATHOMED ITS DEEPER IMPORT.

NATHANIEL HAWTHORNE

Think back to the dreams you had in childhood. Was anything impossible? Apply that same excitement and make some of those dreams realities.

I want to help you grow as beautiful as God meant for you to be when He thought of you first.

GEORGE MACDONALD

IF YOU WANT TO BE SOMEBODY,
START BY CARING FOR ANOTHER.

You will find, as you look back upon your life,
that the moments when you have really lived are the moments
when you have done things in the spirit of love.

HENRY DRUMMOND

EVERYONE FROM THE BEGGAR ON THE STREET
TO THE CORPORATE EXECUTIVE
IS VISIBLE TO GOD.

*I'm living in this world, but I am
not a true citizen. Though I have never
been to my eternal home, I know where it is.
One day I will be there, embraced
with open arms.*

RESPONSIBILITY IS THE PRICE OF GREATNESS.

WINSTON CHURCHILL

THE MOST PRECIOUS THINGS OF
LIFE ARE NEAR AT HAND.

JOHN BURROUGHS

Failure is giving up—before even beginning.
Not everyone can be the best at everything,
but a valid attempt at what God gives us
to do is well worth the effort.

If we have been united with him like this in his death, we will certainly also be united with him in his resurrection. For we know that our old self was crucified with him so that the body of sin might be done away with, that we should no longer be slaves to sin—because anyone who has died has been freed from sin.

ROMANS 6:5-7

NEVER TALK DEFEAT.
USE WORDS LIKE HOPE, BELIEF, FAITH, VICTORY.

NORMAN VINCENT PEALE

Some people come into our lives and quickly go.
Some stay awhile and leave footprints on our hearts,
and we are never, ever the same.

FLAVIA WEEDEN

THE HAPPIEST MOMENTS OF MY LIFE HAVE
BEEN THE FEW WHICH I HAVE PASSED
AT HOME IN THE BOSOM OF MY FAMILY.

THOMAS JEFFERSON

Grace is no stationary thing; it is ever becoming.
It is flowing straight out of God's heart. Grace does
nothing but reform and convey God. Grace makes the soul
conformable to the will of God. God, the ground
of the soul, and the grace go together.

MEISTER ECKHART

HOPE SPRINGS ETERNAL IN
THE HUMAN BREAST.

ALEXANDER POPE

You can see the stars with the naked eye—but you can see galaxies with a telescope. Seek out new opportunities. Think what wonderful advances you might make.

HOPE IS A VIGOROUS PRINCIPLE. . .
IT SETS THE HEAD AND HEART TO WORK,
AND ANIMATES A MAN TO DO HIS UTMOST.

JEREMY COLLIER

"The LORD bless you and keep you;
the LORD make his face shine upon you
and be gracious to you; the LORD turn his
face toward you and give you peace."

NUMBERS 6:24-26

"BE STILL, AND KNOW THAT I AM GOD;
I WILL BE EXALTED AMONG THE NATIONS,
I WILL BE EXALTED IN THE EARTH."

PSALM 46:10

Success often comes in little steps.
Set short- and long-term goals.
Be determined to march forward
despite setbacks.

*Three times I pleaded with the Lord
to take it away from me. But he said to me,
"My grace is sufficient for you,
for my power is made perfect in weakness."
Therefore I will boast all the more gladly
about my weaknesses, so that Christ's power
may rest on me. That is why, for Christ's sake,
I delight in weaknesses, in insults,
in hardships, in persecutions, in difficulties.
For when I am weak, then I am strong.*

2 CORINTHIANS 12:8-10

GOD'S PROMISES ARE TO BE THE GUIDE AND
MEASURE OF OUR DESIRES AND EXPECTATIONS.

MATTHEW HENRY

God's grace goes before us on days when we'd rather just stay in bed.

Time is constant and moves at an even pace.
No one can alter it.
What we can do, however,
is choose to live in each moment.

GREATNESS LIES, NOT IN BEING STRONG,
BUT IN THE RIGHT USING OF STRENGTH.

HENRY WARD BEECHER

We see the daily needs and problems in this world, and we shake our heads in bewilderment. What is God doing? Remember that God has equipped us to be a part of something life-changing and bigger than ourselves.

HOPE IS WANTING SOMETHING SO EAGERLY
THAT—IN SPITE OF ALL THE EVIDENCE
THAT YOU'RE NOT GOING TO GET IT—
YOU GO RIGHT ON WANTING IT.

NORMA VINCENT PEALE

WORSHIP THE LORD MONDAY THROUGH SATURDAY, NOT JUST DURING A PLANNED WORSHIP SERVICE ON SUNDAY.

*God is bigger than my schedule.
My projects come and go, but He stays the
same. My work is often obsolete after only a
few weeks, months, or years—but work
for Him continues through eternity.*

IF IT WERE NOT FOR HOPES,
THE HEART WOULD BREAK.

THOMAS FULLER

Open my eyes that I may see
wonderful things in your law.

PSALM 119:18

THIS IS THE MIRACLE THAT HAPPENS
EVERY TIME TO THOSE WHO REALLY LOVE:
THE MORE THEY GIVE, THE MORE THEY POSSESS.

RAINER MARIA RILKE

Who says a singing voice has to be good?
Crank up the car radio and enjoy.
You'll give other motorists some much-needed smiles.

HAPPY WILL THAT HOUSE BE IN WHICH
RELATIONS ARE FORMED FROM CHARACTER.

RALPH WALDO EMERSON

Since, then, you have been raised
with Christ, set your hearts on things above,
where Christ is seated at the right hand of God.
Set your minds on things above,
not on earthly things. For you died,
and your life is now hidden with Christ in God.
When Christ, who is your life, appears,
then you also will appear with him in glory.

COLOSSIANS 3:1-4

WE HAVE A GOD WHO DELIGHTS
IN IMPOSSIBILITIES.

ANDREW MURRAY

*Communication with God is a great sea
that fits every bend in the shore of human need.*

HARRY EMERSON FOSDICK

THE QUICKEST WAY TO MOVE PAST
THE HARD TIMES IS TO WALK THROUGH
THE NIGHT AND ARRIVE, ONCE AGAIN,
IN A NEW DAY WITH NEW LIGHT.

How priceless is your unfailing love!
Both high and low among men find refuge
in the shadow of your wings.
They feast on the abundance of your house;
you give them drink from your river of delights.
For with you is the fountain of life; in your light we see light.

PSALM 36:7-9

WHO WOULD HAVE THOUGHT THAT
THE DREAMS YOU HAD YESTERDAY
MIGHT SOMEHOW INFLUENCE TOMORROW?

Rarely can we change a person's mind.
Instead, live by example and hope
that at least a few people are watching.

LOVE COMES WHEN WE TAKE THE TIME TO
UNDERSTAND AND CARE FOR ANOTHER PERSON.

JANETTE OKE

I believe Christ died for me. This is enough to make me rise from my bed each day and give something back—my praise.

WHAT LIES BEHIND US AND WHAT LIES
BEFORE US ARE TINY MATTERS COMPARED
TO WHAT LIES WITHIN US.

RALPH WALDO EMERSON

*Every heart that has beat strong and cheerfully
has left a hopeful impulse behind it in the world,
and bettered the tradition of mankind.*

ROBERT LOUIS STEVENSON

Trust Him when dark doubts assail thee,
trust Him when thy strength is small,
trust Him when to simply trust Him seems
the hardest thing of all. Trust Him, He is faithful;
trust Him, for His will is best; trust Him,
for the heart of Jesus is the only place of rest.

SALESIAN MISSIONS

A YOUNG BRANCH TAKES ON ALL THE BENDS
THAT ONE GIVES TO IT.

CHINESE PROVERB

THERE IS SECURITY IN KNOWING YOU ARE APPRECIATED. TO WHOM DO YOU SHOW YOUR APPRECIATION?

*If given the opportunity, people will use
their abilities for something good in the world.*

*I long to dwell in your tent forever and
take refuge in the shelter of your wings.
For you have heard my vows, O God;
you have given me the heritage
of those who fear your name.*

PSALM 61:4-5

THE SECRET OF HAPPINESS IS NOT
IN DOING WHAT ONE LIKES BUT
IN LIKING WHAT ONE HAS TO DO.

J. M. BARRIE

GIVE THANKS FOR UNKNOWN BLESSINGS
ALREADY ON THEIR WAY.

NATIVE AMERICAN PROVERB

*"Come to me, all you who are weary
and burdened, and I will give you rest.
Take my yoke upon you and learn from me,
for I am gentle and humble in heart,
and you will find rest for your souls.
For my yoke is easy and my burden is light."*

MATTHEW 11:28-30

NOTHING IS WORTH MORE THAN THIS DAY.

JOHANN WOLFGANG VON GOETHE

FAMILY RELATIONSHIPS ARE THE PUREST,
CLEANEST, WHITEST SAND OF ALL.

ROBERT H. BENSON

THE HURTS AND PAINS WE EXPERIENCE
CAN BE TURNED INTO GOOD.
ALL WE HAVE TO DO IS CALL UPON OUR FATHER.
HE'LL KNOW WHAT TO DO.

He tends his flock like a shepherd:
He gathers the lambs in his arms and
carries them close to his heart; he gently
leads those that have young.

Isaiah 40:11

THINK. . .OF THE WORLD
YOU CARRY WITHIN YOU.

RAINER MARIA RILKE

No one is useless in this world who lightens the burdens of it for another.

CHARLES DICKENS

BE THANKFUL YOU DON'T
RECEIVE EVERYTHING YOU WANT.

Encourage people you don't even know.
The world will be a far better place.

*It is wonderful what miracles God works in wills
that are utterly surrendered to Him. He turns hard things
into easy, and bitter things into sweet. It is not that
He puts easy things in the place of the hard, but He actually
changes the hard thing into an easy one.*

HANNAH WHITALL SMITH

GOD'S FINGERS CAN TOUCH NOTHING
BUT TO MOLD IT INTO LOVELINESS.

GEORGE MACDONALD

God doesn't size up a man by looking at his résumé.
His worth is not in skill or even job performance.
His worth is in his Savior who lovingly
goes before him, saying, "He's with Me."

A HOUSE IS BUILT OF LOGS AND STONE,
OF TILES AND POSTS AND PIERS;
A TIME IS BUILT OF LOVING DEEDS
THAT STAND A THOUSAND YEARS.

VICTOR HUGO

THE GLORY IS NOT IN NEVER FAILING,
BUT IN RISING EVERY TIME YOU FAIL.

CHINESE PROVERB

Hold on to instruction, do not let it go;
guard it well, for it is your life.

PROVERBS 4:13

Fill your words with wisdom and confidence.
Then people will consider what you have to say.

GOD'S GIFTS PUT MAN'S
BEST DREAMS TO SHAME.

ELIZABETH BARRETT BROWNING

YOUR HEAVENLY FATHER ALREADY KNOWS
ALL YOUR NEEDS (SEE MATTHEW 6:25–34).

May the road rise to meet you; may the wind be always at your back; may the sun shine warm upon your face. And until we meet again, may God hold you in the palm of His hand.

IRISH BLESSING

*"I will lead the blind by ways they have not known,
along unfamiliar paths I will guide them;
I will turn the darkness into light before them
and make the rough places smooth.
These are the things I will do;
I will not forsake them."*

Isaiah 42:16

MONEY AND POSSESSIONS COME AND GO.
YOU'LL NEVER SEE A HEARSE PULLING A U-HAUL.

GOD HOLDS THE WORLD IN HIS HANDS.
WE CAN HAVE CONFIDENCE IN
KNOWING WE WILL NOT BE ABANDONED.
WE ARE KNOWN BY NAME.

Most of the important things in the world have been accomplished by people who have kept on trying when there seemed to be no hope at all.

DALE CARNEGIE

LIGHT TOMORROW WITH TODAY!

ELIZABETH BARRETT BROWNING

*Is it so small a thing to have enjoyed the sun,
to have lived light in the spring, to have loved,
to have thought, to have done?*

MATTHEW ARNOLD

BE GREAT IN LITTLE THINGS.

FRANCIS XAVIER

God counts you among His best of friends.

LOVE BEGINS BY TAKING CARE OF THE
CLOSEST ONES—THE ONES AT HOME.

MOTHER TERESA

*Whether sixty or sixteen, there is in
every human being's heart the love of wonder,
the sweet amazement at the stars and starlike things,
the undaunted challenge of events, the unfailing
childlike appetite for what-next,
and the joy of the game of living.*

SAMUEL ULLMAN

THE DAILY STRUGGLE WILL MEAN NOTHING
IF LOVE IS NOT THE MOTIVATING FACTOR.
A TRUE LOVE FOR GOD AND FAMILY
CAN MAKE ANY MAN OVERFLOW
WITH THANKSGIVING AND JOY.

The sun. . .in its full glory, either at rising or setting—this, and many other like blessings we enjoy daily; and for the most of them, because they are so common, most men forget to pay their praises. But let not us.

· IZAAK WALTON

TRUTH IS THE BEGINNING
OF EVERY GOOD THING,
BOTH IN HEAVEN AND ON EARTH.

PLATO

The LORD will fulfill his purpose for me; your love,
O LORD, endures forever—do not abandon
the works of your hands.

PSALM 138:8

If one advances confidently in the direction
of his dreams and endeavors to live the life
which he has imagined, he will meet with
a success unexpected in common hours.
Go confidently in the direction of your dreams!
Life the life you've imagined.

HENRY DAVID THOREAU

THE RICHES THAT ARE IN THE
HEART CANNOT BE STOLEN.

RUSSIAN PROVERB

TROUBLES ARE OFTEN THE TOOLS BY WHICH
GOD FASHIONS US FOR BETTER THINGS.

HENRY WARD BEECHER

Great wide, beautiful, wonderful world,
with the wonderful waters round you curled,
and the wonderful grass upon your breast,
world, you are beautifully drest.

WILLIAM BRIGHTLY RANDS

This life is not all. It is an "unfinished symphony"...
with him who knows that he is related to God
and has felt "the power of an endless life."

HENRY WARD BEECHER

THE SECURITY OF THE FAMILY AND FAMILY LIFE
ARE THE PRIME OBJECTS OF CIVILIZATION.

CHARLES ELIOT

This world, after all our science and sciences, is still a miracle; wonderful, inscrutable, magical, and more.

THOMAS CARLYLE

LISTEN, MY SONS, TO A FATHER'S INSTRUCTION;
PAY ATTENTION AND GAIN UNDERSTANDING.

PROVERBS 4:1

YOU HAVE 24 HOURS EACH DAY,
365 DAYS A YEAR,
AND AIR IN YOUR LUNGS—
WHAT IS STOPPING YOU?

Your greatest pleasure is that which rebounds
from hearts that you have made glad.

HENRY WARD BEECHER

I HAVE SO MUCH TO DO,
BUT I KNOW THAT GOD IS MY STRENGTH.
TODAY IS A DAY TO CELEBRATE!

Be on the lookout for mercies. The more we look for them, the more of them we will see. Blessings brighten when we count them.

MALTBIE D. BABCOCK

Joshua told the people,
"Consecrate yourselves, for tomorrow the LORD
will do amazing things among you."

JOSHUA 3:5

"BELIEVE IN THE LORD JESUS, AND YOU WILL
BE SAVED—YOU AND YOUR HOUSEHOLD."

ACTS 16:31

WHEN GOD SHUTS A DOOR,
HE OPENS A WINDOW.

JOHN RUSKIN

The LORD has heard my cry for mercy;
the LORD accepts my prayer.

PSALM 6:9

A BOY BECOMES A MAN NOT WHEN
HE TURNS A CERTAIN AGE,
BUT WHEN HIS LOVE FOR CHRIST IS
STRONGER THAN HIS LOVE FOR HIMSELF.

*Do not be quick with your mouth,
do not be hasty in your heart to utter anything
before God. God is in heaven and you are on earth,
so let your words be few.*

ECCLESIASTES 5:2

*Be a leader whose hands are dirty
not by the deceptive things you do,
but by the hard work you put into the project.*

HAPPINESS CONSISTS MORE IN
SMALL CONVENIENCES OR PLEASURES
THAT OCCUR EVERY DAY THAN IN GREAT
PIECES OF GOOD FORTUNE.

BENJAMIN FRANKLIN

May I make the most of every opportunity given.
May my life never get so busy that
I don't stop and talk with others.

TO GIVE WITHOUT ANY REWARD, OR ANY
NOTICE, HAS A SPECIAL QUALITY OF ITS OWN.

ANNE MORROW LINDBERGH

I CAN LIVE FOR TWO MONTHS
ON ONE GOOD COMPLIMENT.

MARK TWAIN

It is better to heed a wise man's rebuke
than to listen to the song of fools.

ECCLESIASTES 7:5

True contentment comes not from money
or even anything we can hold.
Satisfaction comes in the daily moments
we become closer to God.

ONLY A LIFE LIVED FOR OTHERS
IS WORTH LIVING.

ALBERT EINSTEIN

*Running a marathon takes more than waking
one morning and deciding to run.
Working toward the goal may take months.
Even then, training takes commitment and consistency.
Prepare for life in the same way.*

GIVE A LITTLE LOVE TO A CHILD
AND YOU GET A GREAT DEAL BACK.

JOHN RUSKIN

TRUST IN THE REDEEMER'S STRENGTH. . .
EXERCISE WHAT FAITH YOU HAVE,
AND BY AND BY HE SHALL RISE UPON YOU
WITH HEALING BENEATH HIS WINGS.
GO FROM FAITH TO FAITH AND YOU
SHALL RECEIVE BLESSING UPON BLESSING.

CHARLES H. SPURGEON

Tears are okay.
They are a physical indication that
something is going on inside us.

*If one advances confidently in the direction of his dreams,
and endeavors to live the life which he has imagined,
he will meet with a success unexpected in common hours.*

ROBERT LOUIS STEVENSON

CLEANSE ME WITH HYSSOP,
AND I WILL BE CLEAN; WASH ME,
AND I WILL BE WHITER THAN SNOW.

PSALM 51:7